Stained Glass Crafting

Paul W. Wood

Sterling Publishing Co., Inc.   New York
Distributed in the U.K. by Blandford Press

C 2

ACKNOWLEDGMENTS

The author wishes especially to thank Mr. Burton Hobson not only for his invaluable advice and assistance in preparing the text of this book but also for the photographs, both black and white and color, which illustrate and explain it.

Thanks are also due to my father, Albert Wood, and to the firm of Albert Wood and Five Sons for encouragement and help in developing the various stained glass techniques; to Mr. John Nussbaum, stained glass artist for technical advice on leaded glass projects; to Mr. Charles Z. Lawrence for advice and help in developing the facet glass casting techniques; and to Mrs. Lucy Fitzgerald for assistance in the stained glass projects for elementary schools.

Library of Congress Cataloging in Publication Data

Wood, Paul W.
  Stained glass crafting.

  Includes index.
  1. Glass painting and staining.   I. Title.
TT298.W66   1983   748.5'028   75-26167
ISBN 0-8069-7724-8 (pbk.)

First paperback printing 1983

Copyright © 1971, 1967 by Sterling Publishing Co., Inc.
Two Park Avenue, New York, N.Y. 10016
Distributed in Australia by Oak Tree Press Co., Ltd.
P.O. Box K514 Haymarket, Sydney 2000, N.S.W.
Distributed in the United Kingdom by Blandford Press
Link House, West Street, Poole, Dorset BH15 1LL, England
Distributed in Canada by Oak Tree Press Ltd.
% Canadian Manda Group, 215 Lakeshore Boulevard East
Toronto, Ontario M5A 3W9
Manufactured in the United States of America
All rights reserved

CONTENTS

DEDICATION

To my wife Jacqueline, without whose loving understanding this book would never have been possible.

SUPPLIES

Professional stained glass supply houses will handle large-size orders and some craft supply houses carry stock of stained glass materials for the hobbyist. Commercial stained glass studios will often sell supplies in small quantities to individual craftsmen. A free catalog of materials and equipment is available by mail from Whittemore-Durgin Glass Co., Box 2065 AB, Hanover, Mass. 02339.

BEFORE YOU BEGIN

The ancient craft of stained glass with all its shimmering beauty is enjoying a renaissance today, bringing new light and color not only to modern churches and temples, but also to commercial buildings and into private homes.

This book shows in simple, easy-to-follow steps how you can create your own works of art with this beautiful transparent material. Beginning with a simple bonded glass panel, you start working with stained glass right away as you are simultaneously introduced to the materials and techniques of the craft. Progressively more difficult projects develop your skill and give you a chance to exercise your creativity. Included are all the instructions necessary to create complete leaded glass windows in the time-renowned traditional manner but, in addition, there are projects in the new "facet glass" technique,

and other modern methods and applications.

Each project is described clearly with the exact procedure outlined in the text and the different steps illustrated with diagrams and photographs. Patterns are shown for each project, but you are free to use your own creative talent and original designs in constructing your stained glass project.

Tools and materials are introduced as needed at the beginning of each project. In the early projects each step is spelled out completely. As you go on, the basic instructions are not repeated, but you learn some new skill or technique or get some design hints from each project.

A special section of this book is devoted to group projects for use in school, church and youth organizations. These group projects have been tried and tested under actual school conditions.

In planning a project, try various small designs on scrap paper and then sketch the final design full size on a sheet of white paper.

Cut glass on a flat surface that is sturdy enough to allow bearing down. When the glass cutter is scoring properly it will make an even, biting sound. Keep kerosene, used for lubricating the cutter wheel, in a small container near where you are cutting.

Glass will snap off evenly when the scored line is placed slightly beyond and parallel to the edge of the work table.

BONDED GLASS PANEL
FOR HOME WINDOW

Materials Checklist

All you need to begin are:
Pane of window glass
Smaller pieces of stained glass
Glass cutter
Transparent epoxy glue

Using the new epoxy glues, we will begin by making an attractive panel the size of a window pane by bonding stained glass shapes to a piece of clear window glass.

First select the stained glass for your panel by holding pieces of various colors up to the window to see the appearance with light coming through. The color effect is often quite different than when seen against a solid surface.

Now sketch your design out full size on a sheet of white paper. Use charcoal, crayon or a dark pencil, because the outline must be dark enough to show through when you later cut colored glass directly over this pattern. The outside dimensions of your design must, of course, be limited to the size of the pane of clear glass you have selected.

With the epoxy bond technique you can use two or more layers of stained glass, but the pieces of the upper layer must fit within

the shape immediately below so that they can be glued down properly.

In making your design and choosing your glass for the upper layer, remember that using two different-color pieces of glass, one on top of the other, gives the same effect as mixing paints—blue and yellow appear as green, red and blue as purple, and yellow and red as orange. Study a color wheel if you are not familiar with primary, complementary and mixed colors.

Straight line cuts are the easiest to make, so you will find it best to use rectangular shapes for your first projects. If you do use curved shapes, be sure they are outside curves (convex) and make them as gently sloped as possible. Also try to avoid having to cut pieces less than one inch wide.

To cut stained glass, you first score it with a cutter and then break it along the scored line. To begin cutting, lay a sheet of

colored glass directly over the pattern for the largest piece of that color. Try to use the existing edges of the glass whenever possible. Now, score the glass, following the pattern underneath. Hold the cutter with the wheel pressed downward against the glass, and with the notched edge of the cutter towards you. The ball end of the cutter goes between your first two fingers: your thumb and index finger should be in position to bear down on the shoulders of the cutter. Dipping the

To cut off a narrow piece, tap along under the scored line holding the glass near the surface of the table so that when the glass piece breaks off it will not shatter.

When you break off a very thin piece of glass, use the notch on the side of the glass cutter nearest in size to the thickness of the glass you are cutting. ⟶

wheel in kerosene or turpentine occasionally will lubricate it and make your job easier.

Be sure you have placed the pattern and glass on a flat, sturdy surface. Bear down firmly with the cutter wheel beginning at the edge away from you. Draw the cutter towards you steadily, maintaining the down-

Break off any uneven protrusions of glass with very small bites of the teeth of the glass cutter. Check the colors of the overlapping pieces of glass as you go along to be sure the effect is what ⟵ you want.

In making a bonded panel, the clear epoxy glue must be brushed on in a thin, even film. The working time of epoxy glue is short, so be sure all of your glass pieces are properly cut and ready before you begin spreading the glue.

ward pressure all the way to the other edge. Bear down hard enough so that the scoring shows clearly on the glass, but remember you are only scoring the glass, not trying to cut all the way through it!

After the glass has been scored, you are ready to break it. If you are breaking the glass along a straight line and if you have enough glass to hold it firmly on both sides of the line, hold the pattern piece flat against the table with one hand with the scored line along or slightly beyond the edge. Grasp the excess glass firmly with your other hand and snap downward. The glass will break off along the scored line.

To cut off pieces less than one inch wide, score the glass as above, but break it off by tapping from below with the cutter along the length of the scored line. Keep tapping from edge to edge until the glass breaks off along the scored line. Curved cuts are scored in the same manner and also broken by tapping. Cut very thin pieces by first scoring the glass, then breaking off the piece using one of the notches on the side of the glass cutter. Uneven protrusions of glass along the cut edge can be smoothed off by working away at them with the notched teeth of the cutter. (This is called grozing.)

With a reasonable amount of care, you

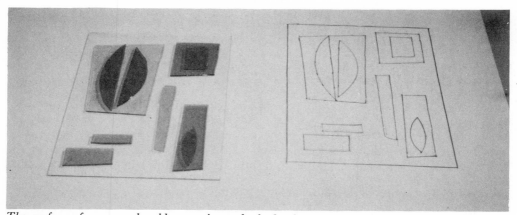

The surface of your work table must be perfectly level not only when glueing the stained glass pieces to the clear glass base but also while the epoxy is hardening. Otherwise, some pieces may slide out of position.

The finished bonded glass panel is attractive with the light coming through it as in a window or when casting reflections on to another surface.

can handle, cut, and assemble stained glass with little danger of cutting yourself. Sensible precautions will help avoid accidents. Do not put away glass with sharp projections pointing out. Professional stained glass craftsmen dull the edges by scraping the edge of a scrap piece of glass along them. Have a scrap box handy for the disposal of small pieces when you are cutting.

When all of the pieces for your panel have been cut, check your colors once more against the light, especially where you have overlapping pieces, to be sure you will get the color effect you want. Now put the pane of clear glass down on top of the pattern and brush on clear epoxy glue over the area where the stained glass is to go, and only that area. Following the pattern, lay the pieces of stained glass in place. Repeat the same procedure with your second layer if you have one. For each bonding (glueing), lay the glass on a flat surface to keep the pieces from slipping out of place before the cement hardens.

Epoxy glue comes in two tubes or jars, one the cement or "base" and the other the hardener or "reactor." Follow the manufacturer's instructions for mixing and hardening time and you will have a clear, strong, permanent bond. When using epoxy, work in a ventilated area. A few people have skin which is sensitive to epoxy materials but you can wear gloves if this applies to you.

The finished bonded glass panel may be installed directly against an existing window pane. A thin bead of putty around the edge of the glass panel will hold it securely in place.

HANGING PENDANTS (MOBILES) OF STAINED GLASS

Materials Checklist

(In addition to those used previously)
"U"-shaped lead came, $\frac{3}{16}''$ wide
Soldering iron
Lead solder
Flux (oleic acid or equivalent)
Small glue brush for flux
Thin wire
Small, flat piece of copper
Rosin

To draw a full-size plan, hold the glass with one hand as you outline its shape with a pencil.

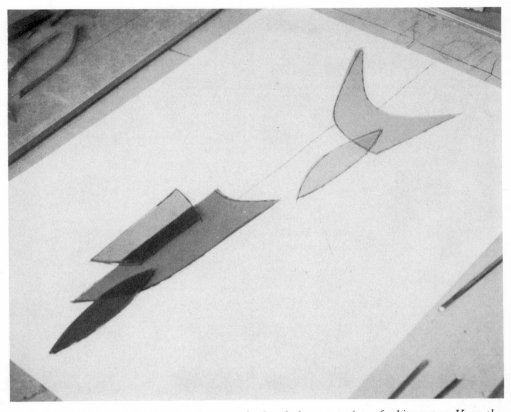

Plan a pendant by arranging free-form shapes of colored glass on a piece of white paper. Vary the design by using some large shapes and balancing them with some smaller shapes.

In constructing a mobile, you can take advantage of odd shapes of glass from your scrap box or any interesting pieces left over from your other projects.

A simple free-form design, suggested by the shapes of the scrap pieces themselves, can be arranged without a preliminary sketch. Place various shapes together on your work table in different arrangements until the effect is pleasing. Each piece must touch at least one other piece as you will eventually be joining them together with solder. You can, of course, cut new pieces to add to your design or recut any pieces to improve the arrangement.

When you have six or seven pieces that look attractive, tape them together with cellophane tape and hold the arrangement up to the light to judge the color effect. It is considered good practice to select your larger pieces from the subtle range of colors, reserving the brilliant rubies and emeralds

13

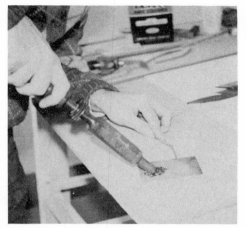

Use plenty of solder while tinning the tip of the soldering iron.

for the smaller accent pieces. Now lay the pieces back down on a sheet of paper and, before removing the tape, outline each shape of glass with a pencil to record their relative positions.

If you have a new soldering iron, the copper tip must be "tinned" before you can use it. If this is the case, plug in the iron and bring it up to "hot" (6–8 minutes). Sprinkle rosin on the flat piece of copper and rub the tip of the iron into the rosin, at the same time holding the solder next to the tip. The solder will flow on making the tip shiny. If, after repeated use, your soldering iron tip becomes rough and corroded, file it down to the copper base and repeat the above procedure.

After removing the cellophane tape, enclose each piece of glass separately in

To make "U"-shaped came out of standard "H"-shaped came, trim the flanges off of one side with a mat knife.

14

To make an even joint, trim the lead with a knife at the corners of each glass piece.

$\frac{3}{16}''$ "U"-shaped lead. If "U"-shaped lead is not available, you can trim off the flanges on one side of some standard $\frac{1}{4}''$ lead came.

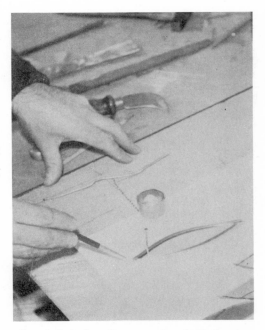

Bend a piece of lead around one of the glass shapes. At the corners of the glass piece fit the end of one lead neatly into the open side of the lead that it meets. Press the lead down on the glass firmly. Now you are ready to solder the joints.

The first step in actually soldering the joints is to use your brush to put a drop or two of flux at the point where two pieces come together. Now touch the hot iron tip to the joint and simultaneously touch the solder to the tip. The solder will run across the joint, bonding it together. With a little practice, you will learn to use the minimum amount of solder necessary to form a bond, avoiding unsightly big bubbles of solder.

Each separate piece of glass may now be joined to the adjacent piece at the point

One-inch lath nails are used to hold the pieces of leaded glass while brushing on flux and soldering the joints.

15

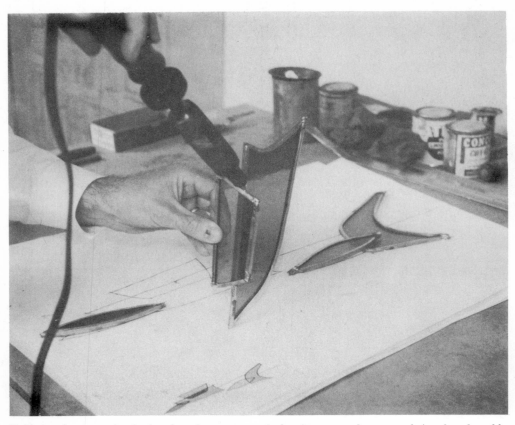

Hold the pieces together by hand at the proper angle for the two or three seconds it takes the solder to harden.

where the leads meet. To give a three-dimensional character to the finished mobile, solder the pieces at an angle to each other. Follow the same procedure as with soldering the joints.

SOLDERING TIPS:

The temperature of the iron must be watched carefully. At the correct heat a piece of solder held against the tip will melt readily. If the iron becomes too hot it will melt the lead came; if too cool it will not melt the solder. You can try your soldering iron on scrap pieces of lead to test the temperature.

Don't use too short a piece of solder as it will be uncomfortably hot near the iron tip and you unnecessarily run the risk of burning your fingers.

Keep your soldering iron unplugged and resting on its metal support when not in use.

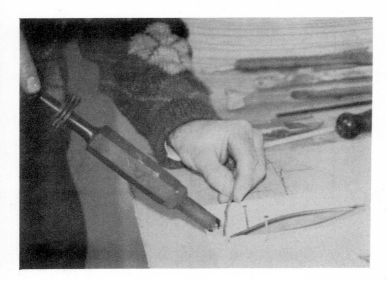

Be sure to solder both sides of the joints of each leaded glass piece.

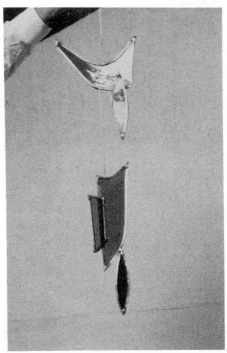

To finish your mobile, wipe off any excess flux or dirt with a damp cloth. Solder a hanging wire to the top lead strip of the topmost piece of glass. Hang your pendant near a light source and as it revolves it will reflect a constantly changing pattern of color on to the walls of the room.

Solder the hanging wires in the proper position for balancing the different parts of the mobile.

KINDS OF STAINED GLASS

You will soon notice how varied different pieces of glass are in texture, color, thickness, degree of transparency, etc. Some types of glass are easier to cut than others, and each produces its own artistic effect. In selecting glass for your different projects, bear in mind the type of glass that is most appropriate for the particular use.

Here are some suggestions:

For door panels, room dividers or other areas of glass where it is desirable to see through the glass, choose "antique" glass (modern glass made by the old handblown method) for its clarity and transparency.

For windows you do not want anyone to see through, use a denser, more translucent glass such as seedy antique, marine or cathedral glass.

For areas that receive a lot of sun, a glass with deep dense color is recommended.

For windows that receive a minimum of light, use light colored textured glass. The texture helps it hold the light.

Here are the names of the more common types of glass:

1. Antique handblown glass, usually English or European.

2. English Streaky (a beautiful textured glass with color variations).

3. Blenko glass, an American handblown glass.

4. Cathedral glass—a rolled glass with heavy regular texture.

5. Opalescent glass—used a great deal about 50 years ago, a vari-colored translucent glass.

6. Rondels—round pieces of glass with a swirl in the middle.

7. Flashed glass—refers to glass with one color over another color, used for acid etching. One side is very smooth; the opposite side is the one to score when cutting.

8. Marine Antique—an American rolled glass in light colors.

9. Seedy Antique—blown glass with little bubbles trapped inside.

Clear glass is basically melted sand. Color is acquired from different metallics mixed with the molten glass before it is blown into sheets. For example, gold is used to produce the beautiful rubies from France (hence the higher cost), cobalt and ultramarine for blues, uranium and copper for green titanium for yellow, etc.

A popular belief concerning stained glass is that the art of producing certain colors is lost. This just is not so and there are many companies all over the world which produce glass that is in every way equivalent to the glass used in the great cathedrals.

The color relationships of various pieces of stained glass can be most easily seen by placing them on a light box.

A SIMPLE LIGHT BOX

An easily made light box will be useful as you progress through the various projects in this book. It is helpful in visualizing the color effect of the glass without holding the individual pieces up to the light. And when painting on glass or cutting to pattern a light box enables you to see the design you are following whether the glass is light or dark in color.

First construct a box out of wood 4″ deep, 24″ wide, 30″ long. The top edge should be rabbeted out (grooved) to a $\frac{1}{4}$″ depth to hold the top piece of glass.

Paint the inside of the box white to intensify and disperse the light. Mount two fluorescent tubes or incandescent light sockets approximately 6″ in from either side of the box and run a cord out from the bottom. A piece of $\frac{1}{4}$″ frosted plate glass the correct size should then be placed on the top. If you cannot obtain frosted glass easily, use clear glass and spray with enamel frosting on the *under* side of the glass. The light box provides a luminous surface on which to see your colors.

19

GLASS SANDWICH PANEL

Materials Checklist
(In addition to materials previously used)
Black epoxy paint

In this project you will create a panel of stained glass to fit full size over a small window. The bathroom window is often a practical selection. The sandwich technique produces a panel that approximates the appearance of stained and leaded glass.

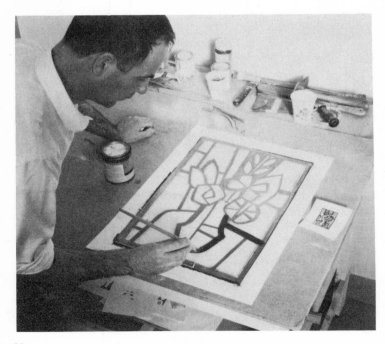

Use a long-haired bristle brush for painting in the black simulated lead lines.

Hold the panel up against a light background to check the opacity of the black lines.

After you select the window you wish to cover, cut two pieces of clear glass to fit into the window opening allowing $\frac{5}{8}''$ clearance all round for a wood frame. Using the size of the clear glass as a guide, draw a rectangle on white paper. Now freely design a pattern of flowers and leaves using black tempera paint or black "Magic Marker" for the basic design lines. Use a variety of thick and thin lines, but do not have too many small pieces as it will complicate your cutting. Medieval stained glass windows had many thick dark lines which served to separate the colors and set them off like jewels. Avoid "in curves" in your design and think of the shapes of the different pieces of glass. A free flowing line is desirable. On your pattern, indicate in tempera or water-

To simplify the color scheme and the glass cutting, a single piece can be cut to cover several of the smaller design segments.

color the colors you wish to use to fill in the spaces within the black lines.

You are ready now to paint the black lines on one pane using the black epoxy paint. These are painted on the back side of the first piece of clear glass. To do this accurately, place your pattern face down on your light box and this will give you a reverse image. Place one of the pieces of clear glass over the drawing and paint in black lines using the drawing as a guide. Paint as heavily and as opaquely as possible. If the first coat is not completely opaque, allow it to dry and then paint a second coat.

The next step is to cut the stained glass pieces. Use your drawing (not in reverse) as a guide for color and pattern and carefully cut your glass so that it overlaps the black paint areas. You have a certain amount of leeway here as the black paint will cover any irregularity in the cutting. *Important note—* select glass that is all of about the same thickness.

Glue cut pieces of glass with clear epoxy glue to reverse side. With clear epoxy glue, fasten the cut pieces of colored glass to the sheet of glass with the painted-on lines (glue to the painted side). Since there will be a

To cut a deep curve successfully, score two more gradual curves next to the deep curve.

←

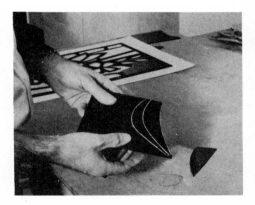

With your glass cutter tap out the first curved piece of glass.

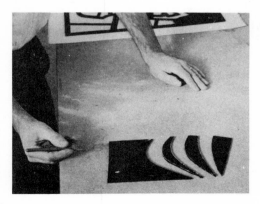

Each curve is tapped out until final deep curve is reached. Any curve sharper than this would require two pieces of glass joined by a lead at the sharpest part of the curve.

backing piece, it is not necessary to cover the entire cut piece with glue—only where the edges overlap the black epoxy lines. After all the stained glass pieces are glued in place, glue the remaining sheet of clear glass to the back, completing the sandwich panel. Set the panel into a $\frac{1}{2}''$ wood frame for ease of handling and removal.

When you have the panel set in a window frame, you will see how the dark opaque lines set off the brilliance and transparency of the stained glass, and what colors do to each other. You will notice the effect called "halation" which refers to the fact that light from the stained glass spills over the black lines making the lines appear narrower than you might expect. You will also notice that adjacent colors tend to blend, creating a third color effect, especially when seen at a distance.

Before selecting the final three or four pieces of glass, hold the panel up to the light. This will help you decide which colors would complete the color arrangement most attractively.

The finished glass sandwich panel shows how the light and dark colors of glass are balanced in the overall design.

STORAGE RACKS, GLASS PALETTE AND A WORK BENCH

Storage racks for glass can be made from the boxes that glass comes in, by nailing them together side by side.

Partition off a section at the top of each box for scrap pieces of the color above. In the beginning, when you have only a small stock of glass, just dividing your glass into the major colors is sufficient. Later on, you may wish to have a separate box for each gradation of color.

Try to have the storage rack oriented to the window in such a way that when you pull out a sheet you can readily see the color against the light of the window.

A rack for small glass samples called a glass palette is valuable as your glass stock grows. Each small sample represents one of the colors in your stock. By placing this rack in a window you can tell at a glance what colors you have to work with. A color numbering system is helpful, especially when you reach the stage when you will be doing complex leaded projects.

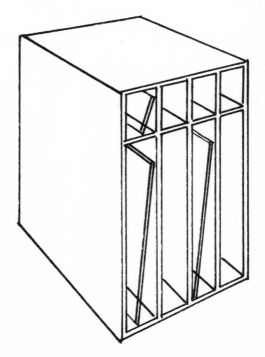

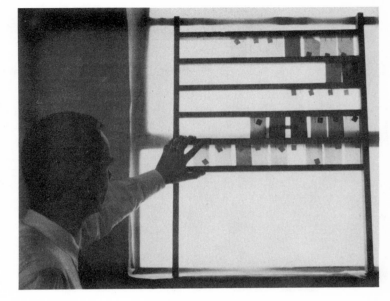

Stained glass samples are numbered and arranged in a wood frame called a glass palette. The palette can be set in a convenient window to serve as a guide to your stock of glass.

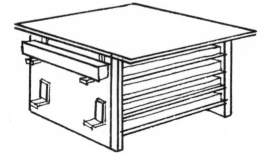

A sturdy table or bench for cutting and assembling your projects will facilitate your work and keep your tools and equipment neat and readily available. Professional stained glass craftsmen often have their benches equipped with sliding trays built in below the top in which they can store separately several different projects on which they are working. The top tray should be reserved for tools. The other trays should be marked on the front, designating which project is in which tray. Trays of $1\frac{1}{2}''$ depth are deep enough for nearly any project, which means that you can have quite a number of trays in a relatively small area.

Angle irons projecting from the side are handy for storage of lead cames and reinforcing bars.

A good material for your bench top is a $\frac{1}{2}''$ sheet of fibreboard. If you have a piece of old carpet available, fasten it on top of the bench for ease of cutting.

25

LEADED GLASS PANEL
FOR ENTRANCE DOOR

Materials Checklist

(In addition to those previously listed)

Several lengths of lead came either $\frac{1}{4}''$ or $\frac{3}{8}''$
Pliers (for lead stretching)
Metal vice
Lead cutting knife (a linoleum knife, sharpened on the outside curve)
$\frac{1}{8}''$ wood strips

Nails
Small hammer
White lead putty
Putty knife
Commercial whiting
Scrub brushes
Steel wool

Using the skills developed in the preceding projects, you are now able to fabricate a stained and leaded glass panel using the traditional techniques of the craft. An entrance door can be made lovely and inviting by the introduction of a leaded glass panel, attractive on the inside by day and colorful on the outside by night.

Since it introduces many new steps, this first leaded glass project is explained clearly and in detail. You may want to refer back to this section later as you do more complex panels in leaded glass.

The technique itself has varied little since medieval craftsmen created the inspired windows in the great cathedrals. We now use extruded lead cames (grooved rods) instead of casting them ourselves, an electric soldering iron rather than one heated in a fire and a steel wheeled glass cutter instead of a hot rod of iron—but other than this the essentials of the craft remain the same.

In planning a large project, you will want to follow the professional practice of making several preliminary designs to scale—1″ or ½″ to 1′ is customary. Stained glass designers use pen and India ink to indicate lead lines and watercolor for the glass areas, as this closely approximates the final effect of the panel. Using a pencil, sketch your design lightly to the above scale. Block in the lead lines and border with India ink and apply transparent washes of watercolor (the India ink will not be dissolved by the watercolor).

Several sketches can be made to try different effects—colors, lead widths, etc. A simple geometric design is suggested for your first project, so that your panel can be more easily leaded.

When you have decided on the final design, you must then enlarge the selected sketch to full size. (This is called a "cartoon" —the traditional name used for full-size detailed drawings). If your design is very simple you may be able to draw it freehand on the full-size drawing, following your small sketch. However, most artists enlarge by "squaring off." This is done by dividing your sketch into a number of equal squares

and dividing your full-size paper into an equivalent number of squares. You then transfer the design from each small square to the larger square. The full-size drawing must be done with great accuracy as all dimensions of the glass panel are taken from it. Color selection, however, is usually made from the original color sketch.

Charcoal is an excellent medium for this full-size drawing. Lines can be easily changed and shifted when necessary—it is black enough for indication of lead lines— and when you are satisfied with the look of it, it can be sprayed with fixative to prevent smudging.

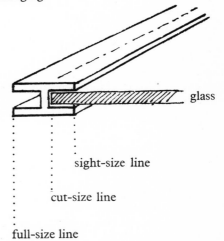

glass

sight-size line

cut-size line

full-size line

There are three vital measurements that go on your full-size cartoon (see above).

1. Full-size line—This represents the outer edge or perimeter of your leaded panel.

2. Sight-size line—This line indicates the inside line of the lead came.

3. To determine the cut-size line—Take a piece of lead came and place it with the outside edge on the full-size line. Where the glass itself will end when inserted in the came is the cut-size line.

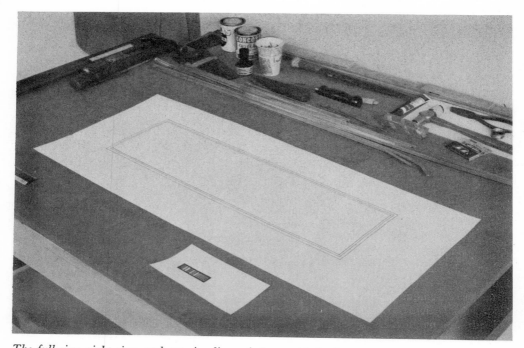

The full-size, sight-size, and cut-size lines of the outside lead cames are clearly marked on the cartoon before the inside lead lines are indicated.

Once your full-size cartoon is completed, you still need two additional full-size sheets —one for your paper pattern for cutting glass and one as a working drawing, to serve as a leading guide.

Put two blank sheets on your table with the full-size cartoon on top and pieces of carbon paper in between. Tack through all three sheets and carbons so that the papers will not shift as you trace the lines. Trace the three perimeter lines—full-size, cut-size, sight-size—first, using an HB or 1H pencil. Use a straight edge for this and for any other straight lines that you will trace. Now trace down the *middle* of each lead line. Press down firmly with the pencil so that the lines

will show on the two lower pieces of paper.

While your sheets are still tacked down, number each individual segment that will be a cut piece of glass. Start at the lower left and end with the upper right segments. Later on when the pattern is cut apart, you will keep the numbered pattern with the piece of cut glass so you will always know its relative position in the panel.

Using your glass palette, select the colors for your panel and write the appropriate color number on each pattern. A convenient color system uses a letter for the basic color followed by a number indicating gradation (B-1 = Blue, light, etc.)

Now separate the sheets and you are ready

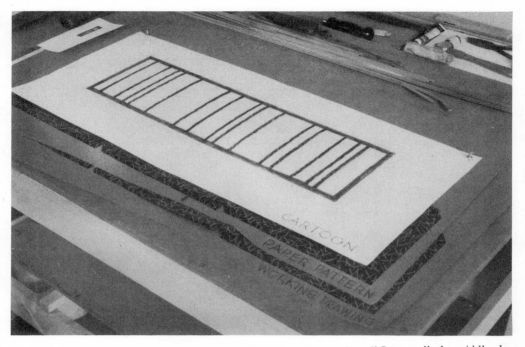

Identify each of the three sheets of paper by labelling the top sheet "Cartoon," the middle sheet "Paper pattern" and the bottom sheet "Working drawing."

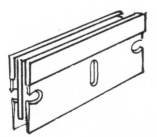

to cut your paper patterns from one of the copies. A professional double-bladed pattern shears is very useful here but perhaps not readily available. Two single-edge razor blades taped together with a $\frac{1}{16}''$ wood or cardboard spacer in-between make a good substitute (see drawing).

The two razor blades or shears cut the paper patterns and allow for the width of the lead heart which, of course, comes between each piece of glass. However, cut the outer perimeter cut-size line with a single blade.

Now cut out the paper patterns and place them in their correct position on top of the second copy, which is your working drawing. Cut the pieces of selected glass, using the paper pattern as shown in the illustration. Glass must be cut very accurately to the paper pattern or leading will be difficult. As each pattern of glass is cut, return it to its proper place on the working drawing (with paper pattern).

The position number of each segment is written to the left on the paper pattern and the color number is written to the right.

Keep the correct paper pattern under each piece of stained glass as it is cut and placed in proper order on the cartoon.

When all pieces are cut you are ready to begin leading. Take the glass segments off your working drawing and place *in proper order* next to your work bench or table. Staple or tape your working drawing to the top of your work bench.

Before lead came is used, it must be stretched to straighten it and take up any slack. A vice and pliers are the only tools you need. Place one end of the lead in the vice. Hold the other firmly with the pliers. Pull with enough pressure so that the 6' length of lead stretches 2″ or 3″. Leads must also be opened by running a sharpened pencil down each groove to force the lead apart.

When cutting many pieces of stained glass, a piece of carpet placed on the work bench makes an excellent cutting surface.

When stretching short pieces of lead came, pull with just enough force to straighten the lead.

31

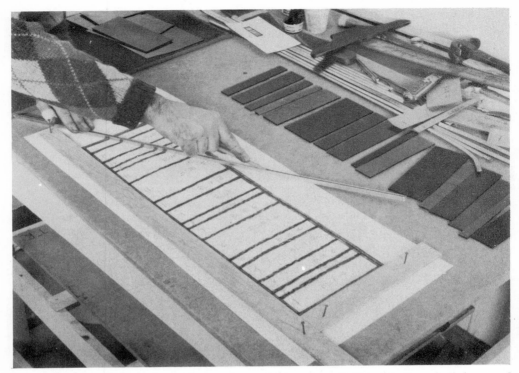

Open the flanges of the lead came by running a sharpened pencil dipped in linseed oil down each groove. Opening will allow different thicknesses of stained glass to fit into the came.

Nail two $\frac{1}{4}$"-thick wooden strips at right angles to the panel on the lower left line marked full size. Start leading from lower left corner of panel (piece # 1). Place the first piece of came against the wood strip covering the lower edge of the panel. Place the second piece of lead at right angles to the first, against the other wood strip. Open up the edge of one came, so that the other one may slip under it slightly as they meet.

Cut the lead came by placing the knife on the top of the lead directly over the heart and bearing down firmly using a slight rocking motion.

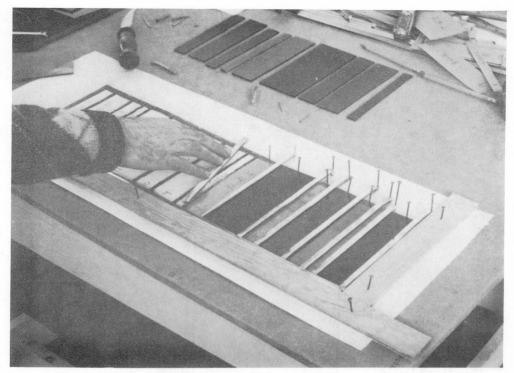

As the leading progresses, use one-inch lath nails to hold the glass pieces and the lead strips in position.

A handy and inexpensive tool for cutting lead can be the sharpened reverse (bottom) side of a linoleum cutting knife. A firm, slightly rocking motion directly down on the lead is the best way to cut. Keep your knife sharp.

Now insert the first piece of glass into the lead grooves at the lower left. Tap it in slightly with the wooden handle of your knife. Next place a piece of lead along the

Trim the ends of the lead strips as close to the glass as possible without actually touching the edges.

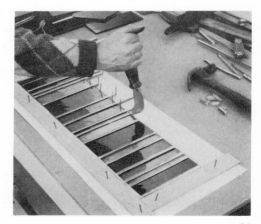

33

top of the glass, fitting the glass into the groove. Now add the second piece of glass and so forth with each piece. Where leads meet at the joint, the end of one can be fitted into the side of the other, or butted. All the pieces of glass and lead are put down in this manner, until the other two edges are reached. Then the two remaining perimeter leads are put down. Any leads meeting the outside leads should fit into the groove. Place $\frac{1}{4}''$ wood strips against the last two outside leads and tap against them with a hammer until everything is firmly held. Tack these last two wood strips down and this will hold your panel for soldering.

Soldering each of the joints comes next. Set your soldering iron to heat and, while it is heating, brush flux on each joint. When the iron is hot, touch solder and the iron

Slip the point of the lead cutting knife under the ends of the lead strips and bend them up slightly so that they will fit more easily into the groove of the perimeter lead.

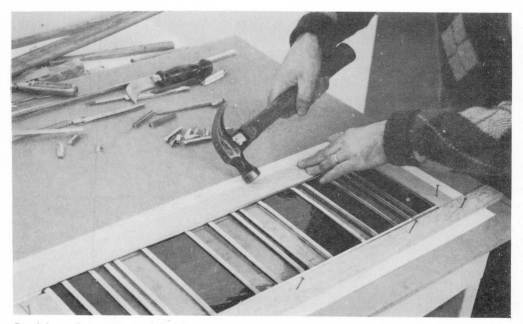

Straighten the outside lead line by tapping against the wood strip before nailing it down on the work surface.

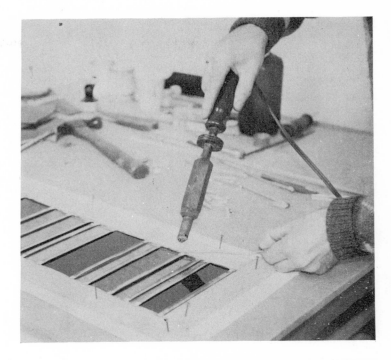

Be sure all of the joints on one side are soldered before turning the panel over to solder the joints on the other side.

tip to the joint simultaneously. The solder should flow evenly over the joint, although this may require a little practice. Fortunately, even joints that are not soldered too smoothly have that interesting "handmade" look.

After soldering all joints on one side, remove the wood strips and carefully hold the panel up to the light. At this point you can, if necessary, change a color or replace a piece of glass that has cracked. Put the panel down unsoldered side up and pry up the lead rim around the piece to be changed. Cut a fresh piece of glass slightly smaller than the first one and place it in the lead. Press the lead down and solder at the joints. When you are satisfied with the appearance of the panel, solder all joints on this side.

The final process before installing your window is to putty the panel. Lay the panel

Press putty into all the openings on both sides of the panel in order to weatherproof it completely.

35

Use a stiff bladed putty knife for pressing down the face of the lead strips.

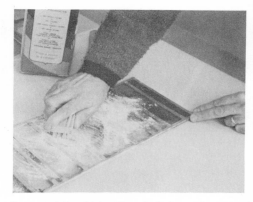

Commercial whiting brushed into the panel cleans the glass and absorbs excess oil from the putty.

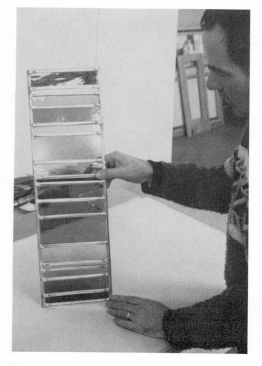

flat on your work table and, with your thumb and fingers, press white lead putty into all the lead grooves on one side of the panel, to seal them. Carefully press down on all the leads with a putty knife and cut off any excess putty with a sharp pointed piece of wood. Repeat this operation on the other side of the panel.

Sprinkle whiting on the panel and scrub the glass and lead with a stiff brush to clean off the remaining putty and dirt. Finally polish with a soft cloth.

INSTALLATION PROCEDURE:

Cut an opening in the door allowing $\frac{1}{8}''$ clearance around stained glass panel. Fasten $\frac{1}{2}''$ wood moulding around the inside of the opening. Run a band of putty against this moulding and press the panel into place. Now nail inside moulding into place against glass panel.

Allow the putty to harden for two or three days before installing a stained glass panel.

STAINED AND LEADED GLASS ROOM DIVIDER

Stained glass can create an effective divider in almost any room in your home. While keeping an open, light feeling, a large floor-to-ceiling divider can separate living areas. A smaller divider, as in the project here, rising from a wood base to the ceiling can mark off corridors or other small areas.

In planning a project such as a room divider, a scale sketch is essential to study the amount of glass and the colors you wish

A variety of curved shapes in the largest section of the room divider serve to soften the severity of the rectangular shapes.

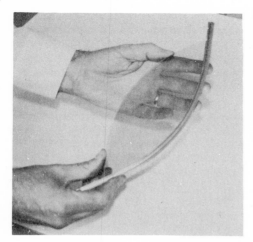

When leading curved pieces of glass, bend a length of came directly to the curve of the glass, trim the ends, and then fit the piece into the panel.

As you lead the panel, check the location of each piece of glass against the working drawing.

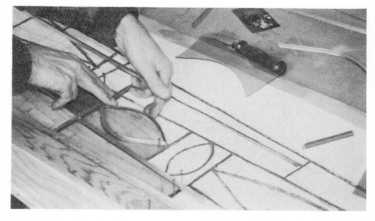

to use. The colors in the divider will affect all of the other colors in your room. The room for which the glass divider in our illustrations is intended has a warm feeling which we are carrying into our glass design— ambers, golds, browns, oranges, etc.

Only part of the divider will be of glass— some sections will be left open, giving a pleasant lightness to the overall appearance. Keep in mind that light, transparent glass—with strong accents of deeper brighter glass

—is the most pleasing in this kind of project.

Follow the procedure described in the leaded door panel project. You may wish to use more free-form shapes in this project so remember to cut carefully to pattern and, when leading, to shape the lead firmly along the curves of the glass. You may also want to try two widths of lead—$\frac{1}{4}''$ lead for fine lines and $\frac{1}{2}''$ lead for heavy lines. This gives an interesting variety to the lead lines, but does not affect any of your fabrication steps.

KINDS OF LEAD CAME

Now that you have used $\frac{1}{4}''$ and $\frac{1}{2}''$ lead came you may wish to experiment with other widths and types of lead. Some available types are:

1. Standard lead cames, as large as $1''$ and $1\frac{1}{2}''$ in width—used mostly for long, thick, straight lines.

2. "U"-shaped came used in edging panels and in lampshade edges.

3. Came with an open heart—used for insertion of reinforcing rods when it is desirable to hide them.

4. Thick cames for use with unusually thick glass or when glazing two thicknesses of glass together.

5. Came with off-center heart. Used for edges to allow more trimming area in installations.

Lead is also available in sheets and can be cut and hammered into sculptural forms. This can be gold-leafed to give a double effect—normal stained glass effect by day, gold bas relief effect by night.

After puttying the panel, you may want to use steel wool on the leads to bring out the silver effect that looks attractive in a room divider. Against window light this is relatively unimportant, because the opaque lead looks like a black line. In a lighted room, however, the lead itself will be seen and the silver finish enhances the appearance.

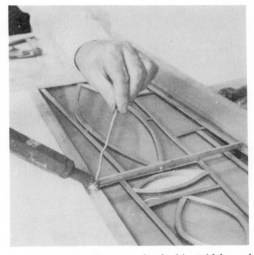

In a stained glass panel of this width and length, reinforcing bars are necessary approximately every 24 inches.

Panels larger than $12'' \times 24''$ need reinforcing bars of steel across the back to keep them from bulging. Set galvanized iron bars $\frac{3}{8}''$ wide at right angles to the panel and solder them to both edges and to each lead that they cross.

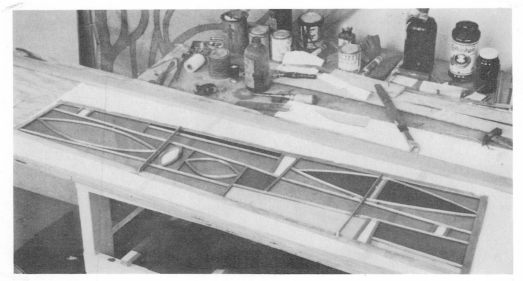

Place reinforcing bars where they interfere least with the design. Solder the reinforcing bars to the panel at each point where they touch the lead came.

Here are the two remaining sections of the room divider ready for installation. These sections are not large enough to require reinforcing bars.

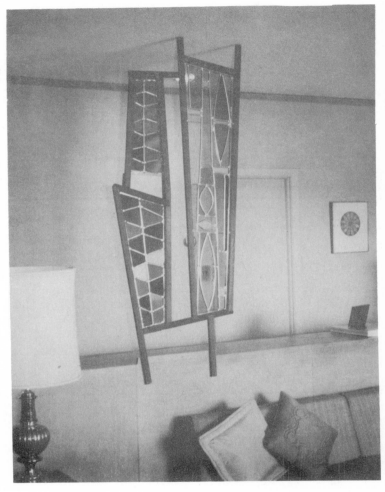

To maintain the bright silvery appearance of the leads in the finished room divider, brush on a coat of clear lacquer.

To install a room divider, a basic frame of wood or metal is necessary. If you are using wood, make an "L"-shaped frame, set your glass panel into the "L" and secure it from the back with a small wood moulding. The room divider frame should be securely fastened with angle irons at the ceiling and base so there will be no danger of its being pushed over. A metal frame can be welded together using "L"-shaped pieces. To mount the glass panel bore small holes in the metal every 16″ or so and fasten the panel in place with metal clips (the same as those used to hold window glass in metal frames). Carefully run a band of putty around the panel to cover the clips and to hold the panel securely in the frame.

STAINED GLASS
LIGHTING FIXTURE

Additional Materials

Light socket, cord, and supporting chain

Stained glass can be used to create attractive three-dimensional objects. A hanging lamp of stained glass provides an area with both color and light. With the same techniques, a lampshade, a lantern, even an unusual waste basket can be easily made.

The design sketch in this case should be in perspective, in order to visualize the final effect properly. The basic form of the fixture illustrated is octagonal and the shading of color ranges from cool tones at the base to warm tones at the top. It is best to use a dense, translucent glass, such as cathedral glass, which will diffuse the light of the electric bulb.

The main wrap-around section of the fixture is fabricated first. Use the same procedure as for a flat leaded panel. Use "U"-shaped lead came for all edge leading and $\frac{1}{8}''$ wide came for the other leads. If $\frac{1}{8}''$ came is not available, plane down the flanges of the $\frac{1}{4}''$ came with a block plane until it is $\frac{1}{8}''$ in width.

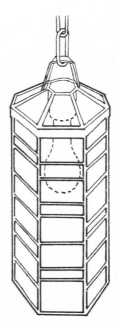

As you add each piece of glass, use a hammer and a short length of lead to tap it into the lead grooves.

All the short horizontal leads in the lamp will be the same length. If you cut them before leading, this will save trimming time.

Use a minimum amount of solder on the joints so that the vertical leads will bend easily.

Bend the lamp body equally at each vertical lead, bringing the ends slowly together.

Place a piece of string or a strong rubber band around the lamp body to hold the ends together for proper soldering.

When the main section is completely leaded and soldered, carefully stand it upright and bend the panel a little bit at a time at each vertical lead until the two edges meet, forming the octagon. Solder the joint where the two edges meet.

Now, using the completed main section as a guide, draw the full-size pattern for the top section. This section will be leaded in the same way as the main section, allowing enough space at the top for the cord to the light socket to pass through.

A curved piece of lead is passed through the bottom link of the hanging chain which is then soldered to the top of the fixture.

Now solder the top section to the main section. To finish off the edge where the two sections meet, a piece of $\frac{1}{4}''$ flat lead (which can be cut from the $\frac{1}{4}''$ came) should be soldered all round, covering any unevenness in the joints.

Insert a standard light socket with cord into the lantern allowing the cord to pass through the opening at the top. Secure the socket with solder. Attach a supporting chain to the top of the lantern by placing a piece of flat lead through the bottom link of the chain and soldering the ends to the top section.

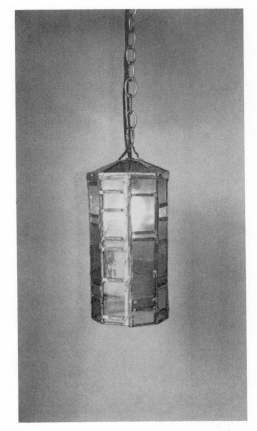

If the finished fixture will be exposed to weather, putty the leads on the exterior of the lamp. This is not necessary if the fixture is to hang inside the house.

OPAQUE STAINED GLASS MOSAIC

Materials Checklist

Gesso or flat white paint
2″ brush and small ¼″ brush
White casein glue
⅝″ plywood or ⅝″ particle board for panel support
Ceramic grout
Mixing container for grout
Rubber squeegee
Sponge and rags

Working stained glass with the mosaic technique is a simple yet effective way to make use of scrap glass left over from other projects.

When small pieces of stained glass are glued to a transparent or translucent surface, the glass allows light to pass through, giving it beauty and dimension. When glued to an opaque white surface, the effect of the glass is clear and sparkling.

For the most pleasing effect, plan to have distinct contrasts between the different color areas, so that your design will appear clear at a distance. Within a particular color area,

however, you can use several shades of one color—the eye will blend this at a distance and, as in an impressionistic painting, will give vibration to the colors.

A point to remember in making stained glass mosaics is that it is best to use glass of approximately the same thickness throughout or you will have undesirable ups and downs on the surface of your mosaic. Also before final glueing of the individual pieces check the color effect by placing the different colors on the supporting glass.

Since an opaque stained glass mosaic does not require light coming from behind it to

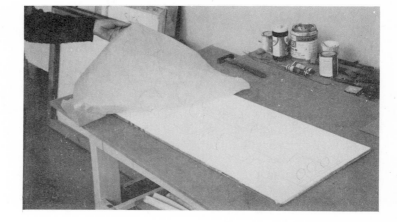

Before transferring the design to the panel, sand the white gesso surface with fine sandpaper.

be effective, any of a number of areas in your home can be chosen for this handsome treatment. The project illustrated here was designed for the kitchen, for a backboard mounted behind a counter oven range. In planning the design, forms appropriate to a kitchen area were selected—bottles, fruit, flowers, leaves, etc.

After measuring the area to be covered, cut your support panel (either $\frac{5}{8}''$ plywood or particle or pressed paper board) to fit the space. Because the project shown was so long and included areas of different sizes, the panel had to be made in three removable pieces. When your support panel or panels have been cut, sand them lightly and cover them with two coats of opaque flat paint (gesso is best for this but any flat white paint will do).

Carefully enlarge and transfer your sketch on to the white panel support, using a sharp pencil to draw in the design. Since the glass mosaic pieces themselves are transparent, keep the panel as clean as possible and remove any dirt or smudges before proceeding to the next step.

At this point you are ready to cut your

stained glass into mosaic-size pieces. First draw a grid on some paper representing your basic mosaic sizes. Two sizes were used in this project, $\frac{1}{2}'' \times \frac{1}{2}''$ and $\frac{1}{2}'' \times 1''$. This is all you will need for most mosaic panels. Place a piece of stained glass over the grid. Score the glass in both directions with a cutter.

To cut a sheet of colored glass into separate mosaic pieces score all the lines, both vertical and horizontal.

Turn the scored glass over, and with the round ball end of the cutter tap directly over the scored lines.

Now turn the scored glass over and tap the back side of the scored lines with the round end of the cutter. Occasionally a small piece of glass may fly up, so wear a pair of goggles for this operation. Since you will be using many small pieces of glass, have a separate box for each color of mosaic.

The next step is to glue the pieces of glass mosaic down in their proper place on the supporting panel. Spread an even coat of glue over an area approximately 4" square. If you try to do more than this at a time your glue will begin to dry before you can cover it all with mosaic. Now, one at a time, place the mosaic pieces down on the fresh glue. Press each piece down into the glue and leave a $\frac{1}{16}$" space between each piece. Keep a glass cutter handy to cut the odd pieces that you occasionally need to complete areas. Repeat this procedure with each different color area until your mosaic is complete.

After all the pieces are in place and the glue has dried thoroughly, the panel is ready for grout. Grout is fine ceramic

When you begin to glue down the mosaic pieces, use them to outline the color area first, and then fill in the rest. This gives clean definition between colors.

To fill in an odd space, hold a piece of glass over the space to be filled and score it to fit the opening.

cement which fills in the spaces between the mosaic pieces. Before you mix the grout, add a small amount of dry color to the dry grout powder to harmonize it with the predominant colors in the panel. If your panel has mainly cool colors, a little raw umber and ultramarine blue can be added. If your panel is basically in warm colors, a

Keep the spaces between the mosaic pieces as uniform as possible to give the most attractive appearance to the finished panel.

Grout only one section at a time as the grout will begin to harden in approximately 30 minutes.

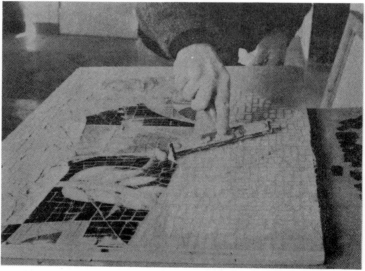

With a rubber squeegee, press grout into the crevices in all directions.

little yellow ochre will help to harmonize it.

Mix the grout to the consistency of heavy cream and spread it over the entire mosaic surface. Push it in to all the spaces with a rubber squeegee. Let it set for a few moments, then carefully begin to remove the excess grout with a damp sponge. For final polishing and cleaning use a lint-free rag. After your panel has thoroughly dried (allow 2–3 days), a coat of silicon wax will seal the grout, making the panel easy to clean and maintain.

50

One section of mosaic grouted, polished, and ready for installation. The light reflections on the shiny surface add to the sparkle of the colors.

Here are the three sections of the stained glass mosaic in place on the kitchen wall. The sections are removable for ease in cleaning the surface.

TRANSLUCENT STAINED GLASS MOSAIC FOR COFFEE TABLE

Materials Checklist

(In addition to those previously used)
$\frac{1}{4}''$ clear or frosted plate glass, cut to size
Clear epoxy glue

The full-size drawing placed directly under the glass provides an accurate, visible guide whether the base or supporting panel is of transparent or translucent glass.

Place the small mosaic pieces together tightly as no grout is used in the transparent mosaic technique.

Balancing small cut mosaic pieces of glass with large single cut pieces of glass throughout the design varies the surface texture.

If you would like a conversation starter in your living room, what better spot to pick than the coffee table! A transparent or translucent mosaic inserted in the top will be sure to catch the eye and add interest and color to your room.

The project illustrated here was designed to fit a central opening of $14'' \times 28''$ in the coffee table top. The panel will be held in place by a moulding at the bottom of the opening. The moulding must be strong enough to support the weight of $\frac{1}{4}''$-thick

53

The finished glass mosaic panel is set into a coffee table top and for easy maintenance is covered by a piece of clear glass cut to the same size as the opening.

plate glass. If your floor color is light, use a transparent piece of support glass. If your floor is dark, a piece of translucent support glass will capture the light on the mosaic and lessen the darkening effect of the floor.

The procedure for cutting the stained glass mosaic pieces and adhering them to the glass support is nearly the same as for the preceding project. However, since you cannot draw your design upon the glass support you need as a guide for placing the mosaic pieces a clear full-size drawing on paper placed under the supporting glass. Use clear epoxy glue for adhering the pieces. Place the mosaic pieces close together, as in this technique you will not grout the mosaic.

When all pieces are securely glued to the glass support, clean the panel carefully and set a clean piece of clear glass (the same size as the support panel) over the top. This provides an easy surface to clean. The entire panel should then be bedded in putty into the opening of your table.

In planning your design, you might also wish to try cutting some of the larger patterns in one piece of glass, and next to these pieces use normal small cut mosaic pieces.

FACET GLASS IN CONCRETE
(Random Pattern)

Tools and Materials

Scrap pieces 1"-thick stained glass
$1'' \times 1\frac{1}{2}''$ wood strips for form
Bag of premixed concrete
Wax paper
Mixing pails
Screened dry sand
Wire for reinforcing

Shortly after World War I a new and exciting technique using 1"-thick cast stained glass was developed in France. The pieces are chipped or "faceted" on the edges and cast in a form using concrete instead of lead to bind the pieces of glass together. This method produces a jewel-like panel of three-dimensional richness. In effect, a wall of concrete with openings of glass is created, the cement acting as a bonding agent for the glass and a structural wall as well.

In America, the technique has been further refined, using epoxy cement as the binding agent. Because of its great strength, the epoxy cement allows great width variation in the cement areas from fine lines to wide areas. Ideal for contemporary architecture, this material has been used to create complete façades of breathtaking beauty.

Since facet glass castings are heavy, it will be wise to keep your first panel to a size approximately $10'' \times 20''$. In order to be able to work properly and to store the casting while it is curing, you will need a working base of $\frac{1}{2}''$ wallboard about $24'' \times 30''$.

First cover the wallboard base with wax paper. This prevents any concrete from sticking to it. Now nail wood strips so that they form a rectangle of the correct size. Within the rectangle arrange random-shape scrap pieces of glass in an attractive abstract pattern. Keep the pieces of glass at least $\frac{1}{2}''$ from each other and at least 1" away from the wood form. Keep the design simple but use a variety of shapes for interest.

When you are satisfied with the arrange-

Small accent pieces of translucent (white) glass add sparkle to the color scheme of a facet glass panel.

ment of the pieces, sprinkle an even layer of screened sand into the form and around the glass pieces to a depth of ⅜″. **Now place** lengths of thin wire on the sand between the glass, crisscrossing your panel. Sprinkle water on the sand until it is uniformly damp. This will prevent the concrete from drying too rapidly and cracking.

Follow the manufacturer's directions for mixing the concrete. It should have a flowable consistency. Using a jar or a tin can, pour the wet concrete carefully into the sand. Fill up the form with concrete to within approximately ⅛″ of the top edge of the stained glass pieces. Do this evenly over the entire casting area. Use a small trowel to even it off. Any cement which falls on the surface of the glass should be removed with a damp rag before it has a chance to harden.

The surface of the wet concrete can be sprinkled with sand, gravel, or marble

One-inch-wide strips of cardboard placed along the inside of the wood forms keep the concrete from sticking to the wood.

To prepare for casting, sprinkle screened sand into the form as evenly as possible. Use a small brush for final levelling.

The work bench top must be perfectly level for the concrete to settle evenly.

Use a putty knife to work concrete into the smaller spaces between the glass pieces.

After the concrete has been poured into the form and levelled, clean the surface of the glass pieces with a clean damp rag.

58

chips. Parakeet or bird gravel which is readily available works very well and imparts a nice sand-toned finish to the surface of a panel. Sprinkle gravel evenly over the entire panel and set it aside to cure in a cool damp place for three days.

After curing, remove the wood strip form and turn the entire casting over into whatever sand remains on the wax paper. Now you are ready to pour the other side. There will be approximately $\frac{1}{4}''$ depth to receive your second pouring. Replace the wood strips around your panel and repeat the pouring process on this side. Again sprinkle the surface with gravel and allow to cure two or three days longer.

Because of the natural strength of the panel after curing, it may be used in window openings or as a divider without additional framing.

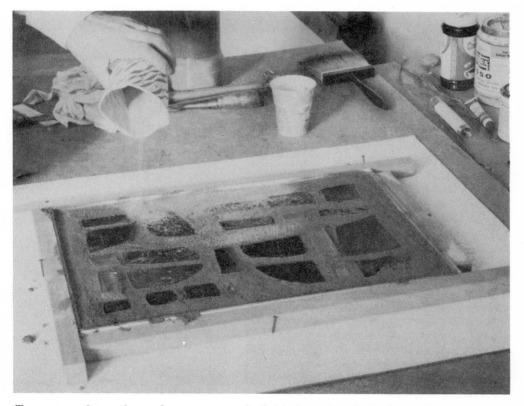

To create an interesting surface texture on the finished panel, sprinkle dry sand or gravel on the still wet concrete. Put the panel in a cool, damp place for curing.

When the first pouring of concrete is dry, remove the forms and turn the panel over for the second casting. Handle the panel with great care until both sides have been cast and cured.

The panel is turned over and the forms are replaced around it. Dampen the surface with water and repeat the pouring process.

The finished cured casting shows the textural variations of all the different glass surfaces.

FACET GLASS PANEL WITH EPOXY CEMENT

Additional Materials

Sheet metal hammer
2″ cold chisel
Assorted colors of 1″-thick glass dalles
(cast pieces 8″ × 12″)
Epoxy casting cement

Designing a small facet glass panel full size directly on to black construction paper can produce a free, spontaneous result. Using white chalk to indicate the design, try for an interesting balance of "black" areas (indicating cement) and stained glass areas. Cut out the paper where glass is indicated—saving these to use later as patterns for cutting. Use pieces of colored construction paper to indicate glass colors, by placing them beneath the cut-out parts of your design and shifting them around until you have an harmonious and pleasing balance of colors.

Using your paper patterns as a guide you are now ready to cut your facet glass to pattern. Exact size is not as critical as it is when you cut glass for a leaded panel. The material itself is rugged and if a piece of cut glass varies somewhat from your pattern, it may produce a happy accidental effect.

For cutting you need a heavy piece of wood, ideally a butcher's block, but a 4″ × 6″ piece of wood about 30″ high will do. If you can find an old tree stump, this will make a sturdy support. Insert a 2″ cold chisel sharp edge up in the top of your block. *Always wear gloves and goggles for cutting.*

The 1″-thick glass comes in 8″ × 12″ pieces called "dalles." First gather up all the paper patterns of one color for cutting. The first cut should be down the middle of the dalle. Score the 1″-thick glass exactly as you score thin stained glass sheets. After scoring, place your hands on the ends of the dalle with the score line in the middle and bring the dalle down to the cold chisel, lining up the cold chisel edge directly underneath the scored line. A little practice is necessary to know just how hard to hit the cold chisel. A good sharp crack should break it cleanly. Repeat the operation to break the half dalle

61

Place colored pieces of construction paper behind the cut-out openings of a facet glass pattern. These are helpful in quickly determining possible color combinations.

into quarters. Try to get as close as possible to your final pattern by this method.

For cuts that are not rectangular, it is necessary to use a chopping hammer. A sheet metal hammer or mason's hammer of fine tempered steel is best. Keep the hammer sharp for cutting. Choose the piece of glass closest in size to the paper pattern. Place the paper pattern over the glass piece. Using the wood block as a base hold the glass at a 45-degree angle with one edge on the block. Chip away a little bit at a time from the edge of the glass until you reach the paper pattern. Turn the glass piece over and put the paper pattern on the back. Now chip away again until both sides of the glass piece follow the paper pattern.

When all of the glass pieces have been

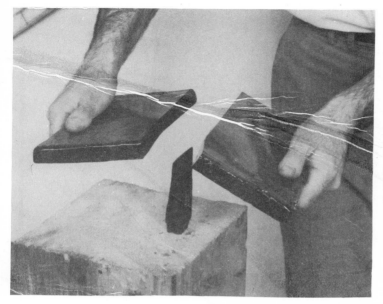

The first cut is through the middle of the glass dalle (pronounced "doll"). This relieves the inner stress of the glass and makes the other cuts easier.

Undercutting the edge of the glass piece is avoided by holding the piece at a 45-degree angle to the wood block.

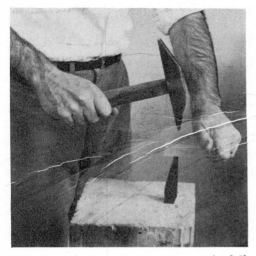

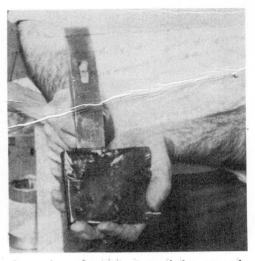

To cut small thin strips of glass, score the dalle with a glass cutter. Turn the piece over with the scored line along the edge of the cold chisel. Hit the glass sharply with the cutting hammer directly above the scored line.

As you facet the thick pieces of glass, save the fish-scale chips that fly off for later use as interesting areas in bonded or fused glass panels.

The basic design pattern shows through the wax paper sufficiently to serve as a guide for positioning the glass pieces.

Color sketches allow you to visualize a stained glass project before you start construction. They help you choose the proper color and shade of glass to create the effect you want.

A

(Left) Following the plan of a color sketch, the individual pieces of stained glass are cut and laid in position on top of a full-size working drawing.

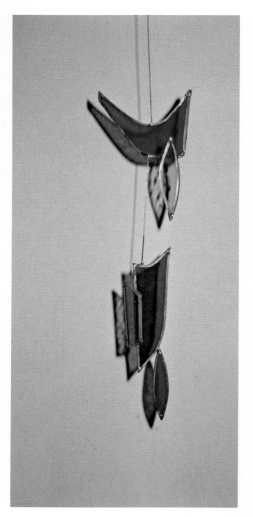

This hanging pendant of stained glass casts its reflection on a nearby wall. The wavy surface of the glass creates an interesting pattern in the reflection.

B

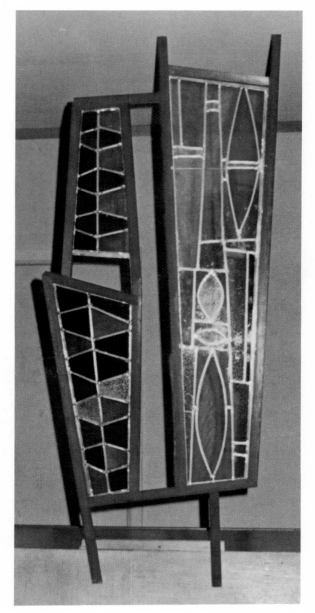

Large stained glass projects like this room divider are constructed in sections, then put together within a wood or metal frame. The open spaces between the areas of glass contribute to the finished unit's over-all feeling of lightness.

C

The "lead" lines of this stained glass sandwich panel are really black epoxy paint.

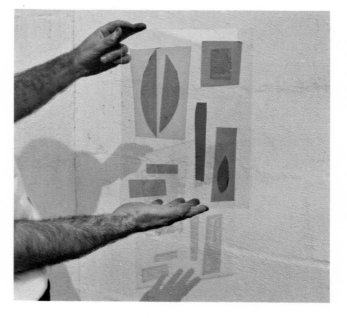

Left-over pieces of glass salvaged from the scrap box can be used to make a bonded panel of free-form glass shapes.

D

These panels are thick facet glass embedded in epoxy material (right) and ordinary cement (below).

This stained and leaded glass door panel was made using the traditional technique of stained glass master craftsmen. In the same manner, an amateur craftsman working at home with simple tools can create interesting and attractive items ranging from small glass boxes to large full-size windows.

This glass mosaic set into an opening in a coffee table top has a frosted glass base which allows soft light to shine up through the glass.

F

Fused glass projects like this tray require a kiln but the actual technique is relatively simple.

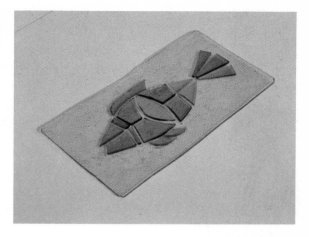

A bright, sparkling stained glass mosaic adds light and color even to such utilitarian areas as a kitchen work counter.

G

Using stained glass and lead came, three-dimensional objects like this hanging lamp are simple projects. The main section of the lamp is first assembled and soldered flat. The soft lead is then bent easily into the finished shape.

H

To prepare for casting with epoxy, fill the facets with plastilene. Clean the edges of all glass pieces with denatured alcohol, as epoxy cement will not adhere to a dirty or greasy surface.

cut to size, you can check the final effect by placing the black paper design on your light box and placing the cut glass pieces in their proper pattern over the cut-out areas. Now decide which pieces of glass you wish to facet on the edge.

Faceting gives added sparkle to the glass. Usually if one-third of the pieces are faceted, this is enough. With too many pieces faceted the effect can be too dazzling. If a piece looks too dark, a facet can effectively lighten it. A color that is too flat can be enriched by a facet. Faceting is done by striking the edge on the face side of the glass. Hold the piece in your left hand with the edge to be faceted facing up. Strike the edge with your cutting hammer about $\frac{1}{4}''$ down from the face and a semi-circular chip will fly off of the piece leaving a light-refracting facet, shaped like a fish scale. Practice on scrap pieces for experience.

The larger can of epoxy is labelled "base," and the smaller can is labelled "reactor." If you mix less than the full amount for casting, be sure to use precisely the same proportions.

65

Be sure the epoxy flows evenly into all the areas, large or small, between the glass pieces.

The casting procedure itself is similar to that used in casting in concrete. There are, however, a few important changes.

1. All facets must be filled in with putty or plastilene before casting or the cement filler will run in and cover them up. Trim the putty so that it is even with the cut edge.

2. Place 1″ strips of cardboard completely around the inside of the wood form. This will adhere to the epoxy and provide the proper depth for the second casting.

3. Follow the manufacturer's mixing directions for casting epoxy. Wear gloves while handling epoxy and use a rag dipped in alcohol for cleaning any spilled epoxy off of glass surfaces.

4. After pouring the reverse side of the panel, remove plastilene from the filled-in facets and clean them with alcohol.

You can display your facet panel so that it is attractive at night as well as in the daylight by building a display light box to fit your panel. Use the same procedure as previously outlined for a work shop light box, but cut it to the exact dimension of your facet glass panel.

Use a palette knife to remove any drops of epoxy that have fallen on the glass surfaces. For the final cleaning of the glass pieces, use a rag dampened with denatured alcohol.

A good device for pouring gravel over the surface of the epoxy cement is a waxed cardboard milk container, or part of one.

The finished casting is a strong structural unit. Several units such as these can be placed one on top of the other (with a sealant between) to fill large window openings or to make a solid divider wall.

FUSED GLASS PANEL

Additional Materials
Electric kiln for ceramics or glass

Fused glass, sometimes called inlaid glass, is a relatively simple technique that can be successfully performed even in a small kiln. Of course, the size of the kiln will determine how large your panel will be. There should be at least 1″ space between the panel and the sides of the kiln. Warpage will occur if the glass is too close to the heating element.

The sketch, prepared in advance, can be drawn full size and will serve not only as a cutting guide, but also as a guide for the final placement of the segments of glass on

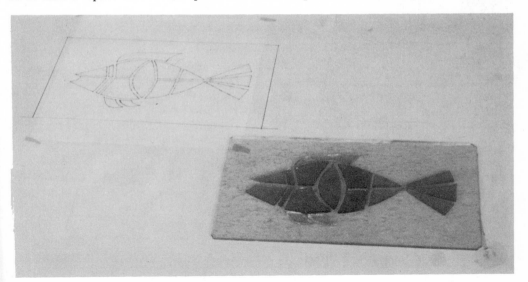

In positioning the design segments of a fused glass panel, leave an even border at the edge of the base panel so that all pieces will receive the same amount of heat.

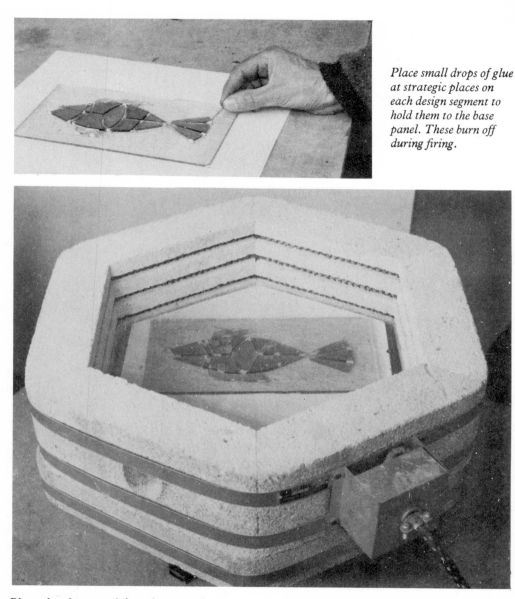

Place small drops of glue at strategic places on each design segment to hold them to the base panel. These burn off during firing.

Place the glass panel face down on the tray in the kiln with the design segments underneath the glass base panel. A peephole for looking in at the glass panel during the firing with the plug removed can be seen on the left side of the kiln.

the glass base panel. When designing for fused glass, allow $\frac{1}{8}''$ space between the individual pieces of glass. When fired in the kiln the glass needs this much space for expansion.

All of the glass including the base panel and the cut segments should be of the same type of glass so that the amount of expansion will be the same all round. This means less likelihood of glass cracking during firing.

First cut the base panel by placing a sheet of clear or very pale glass over the pattern and cutting out the shape. Groze off any sharp edges—sharp points of glass may curl up during firing. Now cut the design segments from pieces of colored glass placed over the paper pattern. Scrap glass pieces can often be used for this.

When all of the glass pieces are cut, position the base panel over the paper pattern and glue each design segment to the glass base, using casein glue or rubber cement. Only a tiny amount of glue should be used, applied with a toothpick to two or more strategic points on each piece.

After the glue is dry, turn the panel upside down on the kiln shelf or tray so that the design segments are underneath the base panel, not on the top surface. The kiln shelf or stainless steel tray must be covered with a coat of kiln wash or separator to prevent the glass panel from fusing to the shelf itself during firing.

A FEW NOTES ON FIRING

Although glass generally fuses at about 1400 degrees F., it is difficult to predict the precise temperature for any one type as different kinds of glass fuse or melt at varying degrees of heat. Glass also reacts differently in different size kilns, so it is necessary to run some trial tests to determine the correct temperature for fusing in any one kiln.

For testing, place a sample glass panel on

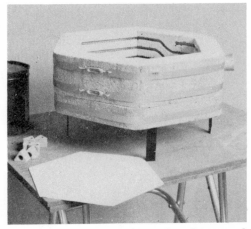

A top loading kiln can be used to fire several fused glass panels at the same time. Stack the stainless steel trays on top of each other with $\frac{1}{2}$-inch spacers in between. The tray shown beside the kiln has been covered with a coat of kiln wash which keeps the glass from sticking to it.

the kiln shelf. Your kiln must be vented during the early part of firing to burn off any fumes and to keep the temperature from increasing too rapidly, a situation which may crack the glass. Vent the kiln by raising the top $\frac{1}{4}''$.

If you use cones as a temperature guide, close the kiln when an 022 cone "tips" and shut off the kiln when an 014 cone bends halfway. Some high-temperature kilns may fuse the glass earlier than this. If you use a peep hole, you can see the bright red color of the glass and see the edges starting to soften. Allow the kiln to cool and then examine the panels. If the edges of the test glass are still angular and sharp after firing, this indicates that higher heat is needed. If there are tiny, needly points of glass around the edges, the piece is overfired and less heat is indicated.

71

PAINTING AND FIRING
ON STAINED GLASS

The range of effects possible with stained glass can be greatly extended by use of painting and firing techniques. The fine details of the great church and cathedral windows were created in this manner. Iron oxide pigments painted directly on to the surface of individual pieces of glass are permanently fused to the glass by firing in a glass or ceramic kiln.

Opaque black lines, called tracing black, can be used to thicken the apparent width of the actual lead came lines. Black painted lines can serve to outline figures and other forms and for lettering. Painted-over areas stand out in sharp contrast to the colored glass when light shines through from behind. Shading, stippling and other textural effects are easily achieved through the use of matte which is paint applied as a translucent veil on the glass pieces. Matte also must be fired and fused in the kiln. Too much use of these painting techniques can overwhelm the fragile beauty of the glass itself, however, so the artist must use them sparingly. Used properly, the painting and firing techniques tastefully and effectively enrich the quality of stained glass designs.

The first step in painting on glass is to prepare a full-size cartoon of your design. In addition to paints, brushes and a palette knife, you will need a clear glass palette and a steady table.

LINE DRAWING ON A SINGLE PIECE OF STAINED GLASS

Materials Checklist

Tracing black glass color (from stained glass supply house)
Gum arabic (from a drugstore)
Piece of $\frac{1}{4}''$ plate glass for palette

Palette knife
Camel's hair tracer brushes, #6 and #9
Wood support bridge
Electric kiln for ceramics or glass

Use a simple bold sketch drawn to actual window pane size for the first glass painting project. If you do a small sketch first, enlarge it to a full-size cartoon, "squaring off" as explained on page 27. A felt tip marking pen works very well for these sketches. A theme of three interlocking bottle shapes with alternating thick and thin lines will be dramatic enough to stand out on even the strongest glass colors. Overly delicate lines tend to disappear when the light pours through the glass, so keep the lines wider than you might think necessary.

Choose a piece of glass in the medium color value range and cut it to the size of your sketch. If the glass is too dark, the design cannot be easily seen; if it is too light, then the painted-on design will be too strong.

To mix the glass paint, pour about one half cup of tracing black pigment on to the plate glass palette. Add one level teaspoon of gum arabic to the pigment. The gum arabic will cause the pigment to adhere to the glass until it can be fired. Using the palette knife, mix the dry pigment and the gum arabic together. When they are thoroughly mixed, begin to add water slowly and, still using the palette knife, grind the pigment into a heavy paste. Continue to add water while grinding until the mixture reaches a smooth silky creamy texture. Now test the mixture for opacity by dipping your brush into it and painting a line on a piece of scrap glass. Hold the scrap up to the light. If you can see through the paint then you must add a little more dry pigment to the mixture.

Use a broad-bladed palette knife to grind the pigment and gum arabic mixture until all the lumps are completely dissolved.

Lay the piece of stained glass directly over the black and white cartoon. Use a wooden bridge (which you can easily make yourself) to support your hand as you paint the design on to the glass. Dip the tracer brush first into some clear water and then into the paint. Now stroke the brush back and forth on the glass palette until the paint is evenly distributed on the brush. Using the tip of the brush, begin painting the design on to the piece of stained glass following the pattern underneath. The brushwork must be done simply and confidently. Move from one area to the next smoothly and quickly enough so that the transition is made before the pigment begins to dry. Do not be too

After dipping the brush in water, stroke it back and forth into the wet mixture until the brush is evenly loaded with paint.

Place the pane of stained glass directly on top of the cartoon and apply paint to the glass by following the design underneath. The wooden bridge can be moved easily to any area and provides a steady support for your hand.

concerned about following the cartoon in every detail. If you put a line in the wrong place, it can easily be removed once the paint is dry prior to firing.

When all the lines have been painted in, hold the glass up to the light to check for pinholes, which must be touched up with a bit of wet pigment on the tip of the brush. When the paint is all thoroughly dry, clean up any ragged edges or trim down any lines that seem too thick by simply rubbing them off with a sharpened piece of wood.

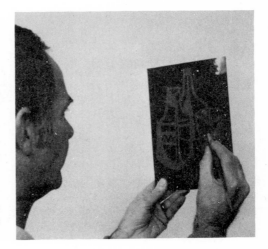

Handle painted pieces of glass carefully while you look for pinholes since the unfired pigment is fragile and easily wiped off.

75

When your glass is ready for firing, place it painted side up on the stainless steel tray in your kiln. Place the glass in such a way that one of the edges can be seen through the peep hole while it is being fired.

Use a pointed piece of wood to sharpen up any ragged edges or to incise delicate design lines in the dried paint.

FIRING POINTERS:

Test firing the type of glass you plan to use with your glass paints or silver stain painted on it is the best way to determine the correct firing time. Look through the peephole in the side of your kiln and when you see the glass glow red and the painted areas become shiny, you know that the firing is complete. Keep an accurate record of all firing times and results with each type of glass and paint. The normal firing time for the kiln illustrated is about one hour and 20 minutes for a full load of painted glass. If you fire in the late afternoon, you can allow the kiln to cool slowly overnight and remove the fired pieces easily the next morning. If you have to cool the kiln more quickly, raise the lid about $\frac{1}{2}''$ to let the heat escape. After about half an hour, remove the lid entirely and the kiln will cool rapidly.

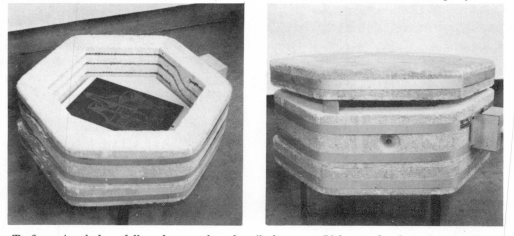

To fire painted glass, follow the procedure described on page 70 but use less heat since you do not want the glass to melt. Occasionally, however, a piece will curl during firing. If this happens, simply turn it over and refire with the next load which will usually flatten it out.

PAINTING WITH
TRACING BLACK AND
MATTE ON A LEADED PANEL

Materials Checklist

Grey green glass color for matting (from stained glass supply house)
Bistre brown glass color for matting

Camel's hair brush 1½" wide
English badger blender 3½" wide
Denatured alcohol (from a drugstore)

Another technique for painting on stained glass is to use both tracing black which is completely opaque and matte which merely cuts down the amount of light passing through the glass. The black painted areas stand out in sharp contrast to the color of the glass itself while the matte finished areas appear to be darker, textured shades of the glass color.

The design chosen to illustrate this technique is a horizontal, rhythmic arrangement of fruits and leaves. Drawing across the lead lines rather than with them gives a

To prepare the full-size cartoon, first draw in the lead lines to which the glass pieces are to be cut and then over this sketch the design to be painted on.

77

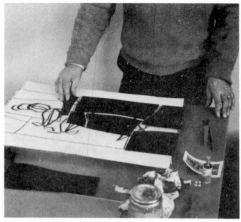

contemporary feeling to the sketch for this leaded panel. Combining free-flowing spontaneous brush painting with matte shadings and textures is a flexible technique capable of producing much variety in its effects.

Cut the various colored pieces of glass precisely to pattern as in the previous leaded glass projects. Carefully place the pieces of cut glass over the full-size cartoon so that each piece rests exactly in the position it will have when the panel is leaded up. A

light box as described on page 19 is very useful here, especially if some of the pieces of stained glass are so deep in color that the cartoon cannot be seen easily.

Mix a generous amount of tracing black and, with a loaded brush, freely paint in the black opaque lines of the fruits and leaves. Be sure that the brushed lines flow evenly from glass piece to glass piece. When all of the tracing black lines are thoroughly dry, you can proceed to apply the translucent film of matte.

First, clean off the tracing black paint from the plate glass palette. Now pour and dry mix equal amounts of grey green for matting and bistre brown for matting on the palette. The mixture of these two glass colors produces a neutral shade suitable for matting almost any color of glass. Sprinkle a very small quantity of gum arabic into this mixture. Now, adding alcohol, use the palette knife to

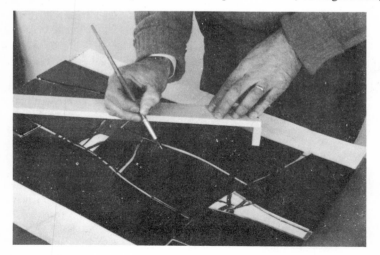

Paint quickly so that the lines meet while still wet or blisters may appear when the piece is fired.

78

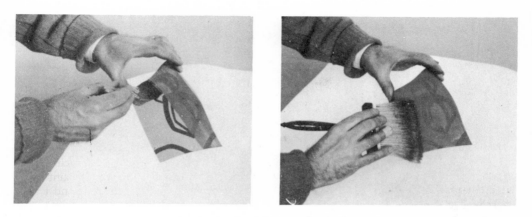

Practice laying a matte film on sample pieces of glass until it becomes easy for you. In this process you first paint on a smooth film of matte with the flat camel's hair brush and then blend it evenly with an English badger blender.

grind the pigment into a creamy smooth mixture. You must use alcohol for the solvent as water would dissolve the previously applied tracing black design.

To be successful, the following operation must be done quickly. First, dip the 1½" camel's hair brush into alcohol which you have nearby in a cup. Then, dip your brush

Old used brushes can be trimmed and used to create textural and stippled effects in the dried matte film.

into the matte mixture and with short, rapid strokes work your brush back and forth over the palette. When you see the paint brushing out in a smooth mixture, pick up one piece of glass and paint a thin film of wet pigment over the entire surface. Quickly, before this film dries, take the 3½" English badger blender and with fast, even strokes both across and up and down the glass blend the matte into an even film. Hold the glass up to the light to check the evenness and translucency. The matte may look a little heavy at this point, but in firing it has a tendency to lighten up.

Repeat this procedure with each individual piece of glass. Be careful handling the glass as the matte is extremely fragile until fired.

When the matte film is completely dry, it can be stippled, shaded or textured to produce various effects. Shading from dark to light is accomplished by lightly stippling the matte with an old brush that has been trimmed. A nail or sharpened piece of wood may be used to crosshatch textures in the matte. A contrast between areas of clear stained glass and areas with a matte film adds

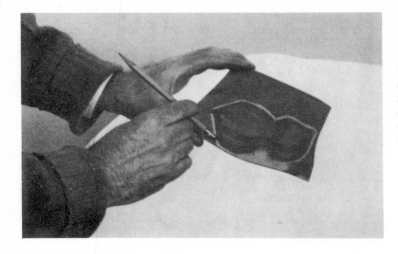

Outlining a design area by wiping out the matte gives strong definition to a form when it is seen in a window opening.

sparkle to the whole panel. To remove the matte from any area, simply wipe it clean with a finger or a soft cloth. For cleaning small areas, a pencil eraser or a cotton-tip swab is handy. A clear $\frac{1}{4}''$ outline sets off the fruit and leaf forms of the panel illustrated. If you remove too much matte, or wish to change the design in any way, just wipe all the matte off and repaint the glass with a fresh film.

An antique look can be achieved by using an atomizer and spraying the matte onto the glass surface. An air brush can also be used for very smooth gradations of shading. All sorts of discarded brushes can be used to produce textural effects by crosshatching, stippling and wiping out.

Be careful of overfiring these pieces, as the matte film burns off easily. If, after firing, the matte film is too light, the entire painting

Painted pieces of glass must be placed in the kiln at least $\frac{1}{2}$ inch from the edge of the stainless steel tray.

and firing can be repeated to give deeper, less transparent effects.

USING A PLATE GLASS EASEL:

As your skill as a glass painter increases, you can take greater liberties with the cartoon as you translate it onto the glass surfaces. Many experienced artists use a piece of clear plate glass placed on an easel with the light coming through from behind. The cut pieces of stained glass are held in position on the plate glass with bits of wax or plastilene. The lead lines can be simulated on the back of the plate glass with black tempera paint. With only a few guide lines from the cartoon, you can proceed to develop the painting on glass with considerable freedom. Just as with easel painting in oil, you can paint and repaint on the glass surface until the effect is entirely to your satisfaction. Faces and features, for example, may have to be painted, wiped out, and repainted several times until just the right feeling is achieved.

USING SILVER STAIN
ON A LEADED PANEL

Material
  Silver stain glass color (orange, intense).

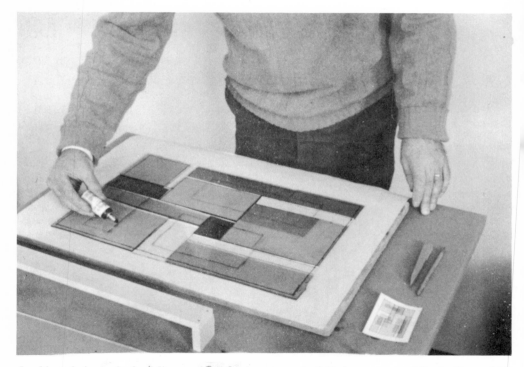

In this technique, the lead lines are lightly drawn on the full-size cartoon while the lines which show where the silver stain is to be painted are indicated heavily. A felt tip marker with yellow ink can be used on the glass itself to outline the area to be painted in.

Brush on the silver stain mixture with a few smooth strokes.

When painted and fired on glass, silver stain turns intensely yellow and is effective in modifying and accenting stained glass, especially the lighter tints. The project pictured is a leaded panel with a variety of rectangular shapes of differently-colored glass. Moving across these rectangles is a counterpoint of silver stain areas. As the silver stain moves from color to color the effects it produces vary beautifully. On clear or white glass the true transparent yellow of the silver stain shows most clearly. On a light blue glass it produces green, on pale yellow glass it produces a deep gold and blue-green glass will turn yellow-green.

Silver stain comes in dry pigment form and, as with the other glass colors, must be carefully ground and mixed with water on the glass palette until it is smooth and creamy. Place the cut pieces of glass over the full-size cartoon and, with a felt tip marker, accurately indicate the areas which are to be painted with silver stain. Using a $1\frac{1}{2}''$ camel's hair brush, paint evenly on the back side of each piece of glass the area indicated for silver stain. When all the pieces of glass have been painted, place them carefully in the kiln and fire. If the color of the fired pieces is not deep enough, paint them again and refire.

ETCHING FLASHED GLASS

Materials Checklist

Flashed glass
Clear contact paper (from a hardware store)
Hydrofluoric acid (from a chemical supply
   house)

Plastic pan
Rubber gloves
Scrub brush
Plastic tongs

In etching glass, modern stained glass artists use clear contact paper as a masking material in place of the wax or asphaltum used in olden times. The contact paper must be pressed down carefully so that no air bubbles are trapped.

Although straight lines are easiest, curved lines can be cut freehand with a sharp razor blade or mat knife.

Another technique, using hydrofluoric acid on flashed glass, further extends the range of the stained glass medium. The result is called etched glass. Flashed glass actually has two layers of color. The base layer is usually white or pale yellow. Over this base layer a thin film of brilliant color is blown. This color layer is often ruby although any color can be used. By masking part of the thin layer of colored glass, the unprotected areas can be removed with hydrofluoric acid resulting in a two color effect from a single piece of glass. Marc Chagall in his Jerusalem windows made great use of flashed glass to produce glowing effects.

A simple geometric design is a good choice for a first project in etched glass. The use of contact paper as a masking-out medium in etched glass is a recent, highly effective technique. After cutting the piece of flashed glass to the correct size, cover the flashed glass side completely with clear contact paper. Press the contact paper down carefully for complete adhesion. Now place the piece of glass over your full-size cartoon. Using a straightedge and a sharp knife or razor blade cut along all the design lines. Remove those parts of the contact paper which the design indicates are to be etched out.

Use a well-ventilated area for the following steps. If the weather is good, you may want to do your aciding out-of-doors. Wherever you work, you must wear rubber gloves. Pour hydrofluoric acid into a photographer's developing pan or a plastic container to a depth of about an inch. Using tongs, slowly lower the glass piece into the acid bath. The time needed for the acid to etch away the flashed glass varies from a few minutes to

Rubber gloves without holes must be worn with a long-sleeved shirt to protect your skin from the strong acid.

half an hour depending on the strength of the acid and the thickness of the film of glass. To speed the process up, you can use a little scrub brush to whisk away the glass as it dissolves. Occasionally pick up and examine the glass so that you can check the progress.

As soon as the acid has completely etched away the layer of flashed glass, remove the pane from the bath and wash it in clear water. It is a good idea to have a plastic bucket full of water handy for this purpose. If you leave the glass in the bath longer than necessary to remove the flashed glass, the

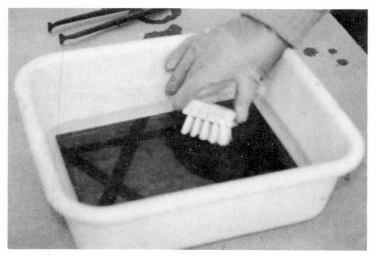

Scrub the glass away as it dissolves, being careful not to lift any edges of the contact paper.

Plastic tongs are useful for immersing and removing glass from the acid bath and also for tilting the glass in the acid to produce shaded effects.

acid will cloud the remaining layer of clear glass. When the glass is thoroughly rinsed, peel off the contact paper to uncover the finished project.

Pour the used acid back into a plastic container. Although no longer at full strength, it can be used several more times. By tilting the glass in the acid bath, it is possible to obtain shading from dark to light. Glass which has been etched can subsequently be painted, silver stained and fired, enabling you to create several kinds of effects and color changes on just one piece of glass.

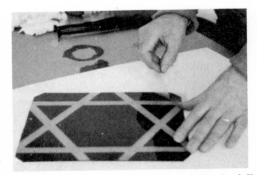

Peeling away the contact paper reveals the full effect of the two-color design.

GROUP PROJECTS
USING STAINED GLASS

The intriguing colors, textures, and changing effects of stained glass are particularly appealing to children and young people. With careful supervision and a few good housekeeping rules, working with stained glass can be a creative and enriching experience for both teacher and pupil. The projects already described in this book or similar ones are perfectly suitable for secondary school art classes, possibly younger. The simplified projects described below are appropriate for elementary school level and have been tested in actual classrooms with gratifying results.

Suggestions for Using Stained Glass with Young Students

Elementary school children may find it too difficult actually to cut glass with a glass cutter, so it is usually best to work with random scrap pieces. If scrap glass is not available, you can easily break large pieces into interestingly shaped smaller pieces. Put the glass in a strong cloth bag. Take the bag of glass outside, lay it on a cement walk and simply hit the bag with a hammer.

Use caution when handling glass, especially when removing the broken pieces from the bag.

A good substitute for epoxy glue when working with young students glueing glass to glass (especially in a glass sandwich panel) is a clear adhesive cement from a tube. Instead of black epoxy paint for the design lines, use a good grade of black poster paint.

SIMULATED STAINED GLASS WITH BLACK CONSTRUCTION PAPER AND COLORED CELLOPHANE

Materials

18″ × 24″ black construction paper
Colored cellophane
Scissors
Paste

To begin, using chalk draw a symmetrical design on 18″ × 24″ black construction paper. The parts to be cut out should be simple and bold, and the black areas in between parts must be thick enough to hold the design together. Using scissors, cut the design segments out of the black paper. Now cut out pieces of colored cellophane to fit behind each opening. Repeat some of the colors in different parts of the design to unify it.

Glue or paste the cellophane to the reverse side of the black paper. A striking display can be made by hanging a group of the finished designs in a classroom or lobby window.

PLASTER OF PARIS CASTING WITH FACET GLASS

Materials

Plaster of Paris
Empty aluminum frozen-pie plates
Scrap pieces of facet glass

Arrange scrap pieces of facet glass inside a pie plate mould. Mix plaster of Paris to the consistency of heavy cream and pour it into the mould. Allow the plaster of Paris to harden. Remove the casting from its mould.

Clean the glass on both sides. Drill a small hole through the plaster at the top of the casting and insert a wire for hanging in an appropriate window.

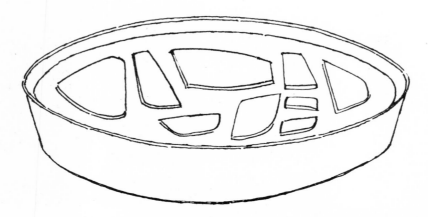

GLASS PENDANTS

Materials

Scrap glass
Wax paper
Rubber silicon sealant

Arrange pieces of scrap glass in an attractive design on a sheet of wax paper. Each piece should be approximately $\frac{1}{8}''$ from the adjacent piece. Carefully squeeze a band of silicon sealant from the tube encircling each piece of glass and joining it at the same time to the adjacent piece. Allow the sealant to dry thoroughly and then remove the pendant from the wax paper. Hang the pendant by running a piece of fine wire through the top edge of the silicon rubber sealant.

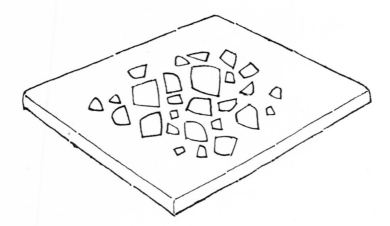

FUSED GLASS
ON A CERAMIC CLAY BASE

Sprinkle glass chips on a ceramic clay tile base. Test fire in kiln until the correct temperature is established for fusing the type glass. Glass will fuse into the ceramic base, producing unusual effects. Oftentimes, glass will change color at this fusing temperature, and these accidental effects can be very lovely.

COLLABORATIVE PROJECTS
IN STAINED
AND LEADED GLASS

With a group of interested teenagers, a more ambitious project in leaded glass can be successfully directed by a creative art teacher. Using the basic techniques described for a leaded glass panel, a school library or lobby window can be enhanced by a colorful panel of stained and leaded glass. Using the school emblem as the central theme and with simple rectangular pieces forming the background, this project can provide an opportunity for students of varying degrees of ability to work together. Use $\frac{1}{2}''$ came for all leading, as this will cover any discrepancies in the glass cutting. Install on the inside of existing windows, so that it is not subject to the extremes of weather.

93

STAINED GLASS—
ANCIENT AND MODERN

The existence of colored glass can be traced back to the Near East where, about 7000 B.C., because of its variety and beauty, it had much the same value as gem stones and was indeed worn as jewels for personal adornment. The earliest known glass workshops were in Alexandria, Egypt, where the craft grew and flourished following the invention of the blowpipe. The blowpipe enabled the craftsmen to control the size, shape and thickness of the glass products.

Under Roman rule, Egyptian glass and glass makers were brought to Rome where early records indicate the first use of glass in window openings, primarily simple pieces of translucent glass set into masonry openings to form decorative patterns.

The advent of Christianity changed the status of stained glass from a minor craft to a major art, and with the decline of the Roman Empire, the hub of glass manufacturing shifted to Byzantium. Here, under Emperor Constantine, the use of glass in window openings for decorative and symbolic meaning reached a high degree of development in the "Great Church of Divine Wisdom" (Haggia Sophia), unfortunately destroyed by fire in A.D. 532.

From Byzantium the craft and the craftsmen spread to Europe, appearing almost simultaneously in France, Germany, and Italy in the 6th century and reaching England in the year 680. The oldest surviving stained glass windows are those of the "Prophets" in Augsburg Cathedral, Germany. They show such a high standard of artistry and craftsmanship that many earlier windows must have been completed in order to perfect the technique.

The existence of skilled craftsmen set the stage for the great glories of medieval stained glass. The intense religious feeling of the times, the architectural developments which allowed glass to be used in great expanses, and the creative genius of the medieval artist-craftsman all combined in the 12th and 13th centuries to produce the inspired windows of the Gothic cathedrals in France, Germany, and England.

Strong vibrant colors, bold use of lead to delineate form, and harmony between the window design and the architecture characterized Gothic stained glass. The emotional effect of these windows is as powerful an experience today as it must have been when they were first created.

After the medieval glories, church art, particularly stained glass, began a slow decline. Windows became lighter in color. Forms and figures were modelled more and

more as in easel painting with a consequent loss of emotional impact. This decline was due to the Black Plague which greatly reduced the ranks of first rate craftsmen and to the Reformation with its opposition to over-decoration in the church. This led eventually to the actual destruction of many fine windows.

The 20th century has brought a revival in the art of stained glass. Distinguished modern artists such as Matisse, Braque, Leger, and Chagall have designed and executed works of great originality and beauty to equal the best of medieval glass.

Churches and synagogues are not the only places where stained glass has been used to enhance modern architecture. One of the largest stained glass murals in the world is set in the front of the American Airlines terminal at John F. Kennedy International Airport in New York City. Designed by Robert Sowers, American stained glass artist, transparent antique glass is combined with opaque flashed opal glass in brilliant colors and striking design.

Today in almost any contemporary building you are likely to find stained glass playing an important decorative role. Area dividers, murals, walls and windows of shimmering beauty, delicate mobiles, colorful mosaics of stained glass—all show that this most ancient of materials can also be one of the most modern.

INDEX